HAIKUS
OF
ALL SEASONS XII

FLORA

MAYUMI ITOH

In memory of

the victims of the Covid-19 pandemic,

and George Floyd (October 1973–May 2020),

and other victims of racial injustice

Contents

List of photographs

All photographs were taken by the author except for those whose sources are credited below.

Photograph 1. Ornamental kale (*ha botan*, *lit.*, "leaf peony")

Photograph 2. Narcissus ice follies

Photograph 3. Forget-me-not in the rain

Photograph 4. Bonsai of Asahi yama-zakura (*lit.*, Asahi 'mountain cherry' blossoms, *cerasus jamasakura*), courtesy of © Watanabe Miyuki 2020

Photograph 5. Asian bleeding-heart blossoms (*kemansō*, *lamprocapnos spectabilis*)

Photograph 6. Princess tree blossoms (*kiri no hana*, *paulownia tomentosa*)

Notes on the Text

This book presents each haiku in both Japanese and English so that non-Japanese-speaking readers can fully appreciate it. The first page for a given haiku (on the left side) shows the original haiku in Japanese, which is made up of a combination of Chinese characters (*kanji*) and Japanese phonetic characters (*hiragana* and *katakana*). In accordance with the customs for writing haiku, the old spellings of *hiragana* are used for the original haiku.

Then, in order to facilitate a better understanding, the original haiku is shown in a modern spelling in *hiragana* and *katakana*. This allows readers to see how the haiku is exactly pronounced phonetically. There are many ways to pronounce specific *kanji* words, and the original Japanese haiku does not indicate how each *kanji* word is actually pronounced. It is sometimes difficult even for Japanese readers to know the pronunciation. Therefore, the simpler rendition of each haiku only in modern *hiragana* and *katakana* will help. Afterward, the identification of the season word—an essential element in haiku—for the haiku is given and some explanations of the cultural and historical backgrounds are added where applicable.

On the second page for a given haiku (on the right side), a romanization of the original Japanese haiku is provided, first, so that English-speaking readers can understand how the haiku is pronounced. The words in Roman letters are divided into smaller groups of syllables, for easier reading.

Then, an English translation of the haiku is presented. It is a paraphrasing of the haiku, rather than a literal translation, in order for it to make the best sense in English. Due to the structural differences in English and Japanese, for many cases, the word order of the haiku might be different from the original haiku in Japanese. It is followed by the English translations of the season word for the haiku and the explanations of the cultural and historical backgrounds. This completes the presentation of a given haiku.

All translations, including those of haikus, were made by the author. For romanizing Japanese words, the Hepburn style is primarily used, with macrons. However, macrons are not used for words known in English without macrons, as for Kyoto and Tokyo. Another exception is that "n" is not converted to "m" for words where it precedes "b, m, and p." Examples include tonbo (dragonfly), instead of tombo; sanma (saury), instead of samma; and tanpopo (dandelion), instead of tampopo.

Names of Japanese persons are given with the surname first, except for those who use the reversed order in English. Honorific prefixes, such as doctor and mister, are not used in the text, except in direct quotations.

Acknowledgments

I would like to thank Watanabe Miyuki, for the loans of photographs, and all the members of the *Hoshi no shima kukai* (the Haiku Society of Star Island, a new name for the Haiku Society of New York)—Esaka Kinuyo, Hara Yasuko, Sakuhara Aya, and Tsukino Popona, especially—as well as Tsuneo Akaha, Kent Calder, Toshiko Calder, Morrell Chance, Steve Clemons, Akiko Collcutt, Gerald Curtis, Martin Heijdra, Hoshi Hiroshi, Ronald Hrebenar, Kumi Kato, Ellis Krauss, Mike Mochizuki, T. J. Pempel, Jaana Rehnstrom, Stephen Roddy, Gilbert Rozman, Anna Shields, Susan Stewart, and Vicki Wong, for generous encouragement and inspirations. I extend my deep appreciation to Gregory Rewoldt and Meg Itoh for continuous support.

Preface

This is the twelfth haiku anthology by this author and
embraces one of the seven major themes of haiku: flora.
The other major themes of haiku are: 1) the seasons and
the weather; 2) astronomy or the heavens; 3) geography or
the earth; 4) daily life or humanity, 5) events or
observances, such as traditional seasonal events and
religious ceremonies and rituals; and 6) fauna. For basic
rules about haiku making, please see *Haikus of All Seasons
I: The Heavens and The Earth* (2018).

This collection is dedicated to the victims of the
Covid-19 outbreak, especially those who fell victim as
medical caregivers, doctors, and technical specialists
combatting the pandemic. This volume is also a tribute to
George Floyd (October 1973–May 2020), who was killed
by a police officer in Minneapolis, Minnesota, and other
victims of racial discrimination and injustice. The protests

against the killing of George Floyd sprang up in many cities in the United States amidst the Covid-19 pandemic, and then spread throughout the world, including Nagoya, Osaka, and Tokyo, Japan.

This collection is also a memorial tribute to the victims of the Great East Japan Earthquake, Tsunami, and the Fukushima Nuclear Disaster of March 11, 2011, and is dedicated to the survivors who still suffer from the traumas of the tragic disasters after more than nine years.

合掌 (RIP)

June 30, 2020

January

Photograph 1. Ornamental kale (*ha botan*, *lit*., "leaf

peony")

松竹梅

　　新春の息

　　　　神棚へ

しょうちくばい

　　しんしゅんのいき

　　　　かみだなへ

季語　新春（しんしゅん、新年を表す）

Shō chiku bai

shin shun no iki

kami dana e

The pine needles, bamboo leaves, and plum blossoms

send forth the breath of the new year

to the miniature home Shinto shrine

Season word: *shin shun* (*lit.*, "new spring," new year;

signifies the new year)

　楪や

　　　二十歳の吾娘の

　　　　　「お下がり」を

　ゆづりはや

　　　はたちのあこの

　　　　　おさがりを

季語　　楪（ユズリハ、新年）

ユズリハ（譲り葉）は、赤い新しい葉が生えた後に、古い葉

が落ちることから、「成長した子に後を譲る」、めでたい木と

され、正月飾りとして神社に奉納される。

Yuzuriha ya

    hatachi no ako no

        o sagari o

The false daphne

    the mother wears the clothes

        her 20-year-old daughter had worn

Season word: *yuzuriha* (false daphne; new year)

The old leaves of false daphne (*daphniphyllum macropodum*) fall after the new red leaves have sprouted in the spring, as if the former give way to the latter; hence the tree is regarded as auspicious and its leaves are used as a decoration of Shinto shrines for the new year.

神馬藻

　　珊瑚の海の

　　　　贈り物

ほんだわら

　　さんごのうみの

　　　　おくりもの

季語　神馬藻（ホンダワラ、新年）

ホンダワラは、ホンダワラ科の褐色の海藻。気胞と呼ばれ

る浮き袋があり、これで体を直立させることができる。楕円

形の気胞の形が米俵に似ていることから、縁起が良いとさ

れ、新年のお供えとして神社に奉納される。

Hondawara

    sango no umi no

        okurimono

The hondawara seaweed

    is a gift

        from the red coral sea

Season word: *hondawara* (*sargassum fulvellum*; new year)
Hondawara is a reddish brown seaweed with airy 'bladders'
(air bubbles) that enable the plant to stand in the sea. The
oval shape of the bladders resembles that of straw bags for
rice, the staple of Japanese; hence it is used as an offering
to Shinto shrines for the new year.

福寿草

　　福島の友

　　　偲び泣く

ふくじゅそう

　　ふくしまのとも

　　　しのびなく

季語　福寿草（フクジュソウ、新年）

フクジュソウの別名は、元日草（ガンジツソウ）。

Fukujusō

    Fukushima no tomo

       shinobi naku

The Amur adonis

    reminisces about its friends

        who perished in Fukushima and sheds tears

Season word: *fukujusō* (Amur adonis, *adonis multiflora*,

ganjitsusō, "new year's day plant"; new year)

The soil in Fukushima has been contaminated since the

nuclear meltdowns of March 11, 2011, to this day.

若菜摘む

　　老婆の背中

　　　　さする稚児

わかなつむ

　　ろうばのせなか

　　　　さするちご

季語　若菜摘む（わかなつむ、新年）

若菜は、七草粥に入れる野草の総称。

Wakana tsumu

> rōba no senaka

>> sasuru chigo

Picking the spring plants

> the child is gently stroking

>> the back of her grandmother

Season word: *wakana tsumu* (picking spring plants for the
new year rice porridge; new year)
It is a custom to eat rice porridge mixed with the "seven
spring plants" on January 7, after eating rice cakes and
other heavy dishes during the New Year holidays.

葉牡丹や

　　淋しき庭の

　　　　お琴の音

はぼたんや

　　さびしきにわの

　　　　おことのね

季語　葉牡丹（ハボタン、冬）

Habotan ya

sabishiki niwa no

o koto no ne

The ornamental kale

listens to the Japanese harp

in the lonely garden

Season word: *ha botan* (*lit.*, "leaf peony," ornamental kale;

winter)

雪中花

　　神の足跡

　　　　埋め尽くす

せっちゅうか

　　かみのあしあと

　　　　うめつくす

季語　雪中花（せっちゅうか、冬）

雪中花は、水仙（スイセン）のことを指す。

Setchūka

kami no ashi ato

ume tsukusu

The narcissus blossoms

follow upon

the footsteps of the gods

Season word: *setchūka* (*lit.*, "flower in the snow,"

narcissus; winter)

老ひ松や

　　雪の重さに

　　　　耐へ生きる

おいまつや

　　ゆきのおもさに

　　　　たえいきる

季語　雪（ゆき、冬）

Oi matsu ya

yuki no omosa ni

tae ikiru

The old pine tree

endures the weight of the snow

and lives on

Season word: *yuki* (snow; winter)

寒椿

　　ニコライ堂の

　　　　鐘遥か

かんつばき

　　ニコライどうの

　　　　かねはるか

季語　寒椿（カンツバキ、冬）

カンツバキは、寒中（1 月 5 日頃から 2 月 3 日頃まで）に

咲く。ニコライ堂は、東京都千代田区神田駿河台にある正

教会の大聖堂のこと。

Kan tsubaki

Nikorai dō no

kane haruka

The winter camellia

the bell of St. Nicholas Cathedral

reverberates far away

Season word: *kan tsubaki* (winter camellia; winter)

The winter camellia is a species of the Japanese camellia.

Holy Resurrection Cathedral in Tokyo, commonly known

as St. Nicholas Cathedral, is a Japanese Orthodox church

founded in 1891 by a Russian Orthodox archbishop in

Kanda, Tokyo.

蠟梅や

　　夢か現か

　　　　長恨歌

ろうばいや

　　ゆめかうつつか

　　　　ちょうごんか

季語　蠟梅（ロウバイ、冬）

白居易（772年—846年）の『長恨歌』は、唐の玄宗皇帝

（685年—762年）に寵愛された楊貴妃（719年—756年）の悲

哀を詠う。

Rōbai ya

    yume ka utsutsu ka

    Chōgon ka

The winter sweet blossoms

    Are Songs of Everlasting Sorrow

    a dream or a reality?

Season word: *rōbai* (*lit.*, "waxy plum tree," winter sweet,

chimonanthus praecox; winter)

Songs of Everlasting Sorrow are poems written by Bai Juyi

(772–846) about Tang dynasty emperor Xuanzong (685–

762) and the Imperial consort Yang Guifei (719–756).

February

Photograph 2. Narcissus ice follies

福島や

　　白水仙の

　　　　海に漂ふ

ふくしまや

　　しろずいせんの

　　　　うみにただよう

季語　白水仙（しろずいせん、ペーパーホワイト、ナルキッソス、冬）

福島第一原子力発電所は、処理した汚染水を海に放出している。

Fukushima ya

shiro zuisen no

umi ni tadayou

At Fukushima

the white narcissus blossoms

are drifting on the sea

Season word*: shiro zuisen* (narcissus, paperwhite

narcissus, *narcissus papyraceus*; winter)

In Fukushima, the contaminated water of the nuclear power

plants has been released into the ocean, causing concern for

the destruction of marine life and the ecosystem.

冬菫

　　古き日記に

　　　　挟む夜

ふゆすみれ

　　ふるきにっきに

　　　　はさむよる

季語　冬菫(ふゆすみれ、冬)

Fuyu sumire

furuki nikki ni

hasamu yoru

The winter violet

one is tucking it

into the old diary at night

Season word: *fuyu sumire* (winter violet; winter)

椿の芽

　　固き契りを

　　　　誓ふ朝

つばきのめ

　　かたきちぎりを

　　　　ちかうあさ

季語　椿の芽（ツバキのめ、春）

俳句では、2月4日（立春）が、春の始めとなる。

Tsubaki no me

kataki chigiri o

chikau asa

The camellia buds

the couple pledges

their eternal love in the morning

Season word: *tsubai no me* (camellia buds; spring)

In haiku, February 4 marks the beginning of spring.

早梅や

　　初孫の顔

　　　　待ちわびる

はやうめや

　　はつまごのかお

　　　　まちわびる

季語　　早梅（はやうめ、春）

Haya ume ya

hatsu mago no kao

machi wabiru

The early plum blossoms

the grandmother anxiously waits

to see her first grandchild

Season word: *haya ume* (early plum blossoms; spring)

クロッカス

　　黄と紫の

　　　　陽の光

クロッカス

　　きとむらさきの

　　　　ひのひかり

季語　クロッカス(春)

Kurokkasu

   ki to murasaki no

      hi no hikari

The crocuses

   are reflecting

      the yellow and purple light of the sun

Season word: *kurokkasu* (crocus; spring)

仏の座

　　小人の国の

　　　　女王様

ほとけのざ

　　こびとのくにの

　　　　じょおうさま

季語　ほとけのざ（ホトケノザ、春）

ホトケノザは、「春の七草」のホトケノザではない。現在は、

後者は、コオニタビラコ（小鬼田平子、*apsana apogonoides*

Maxim）と命名されている。

Hotoke no za

kobito no kuni no

joō sama

The henbit blossoms

the queen of the land of the dwarfs

is sitting on her throne

Season word: *hotoke no za* (*lit.*, "the throne of Buddha,"

henbit, *lamium amplexicaule*; spring)

Henbit has dainty purple flowers and heart-shaped leaves

with big scalloped edges which could be likened to the

throne of Buddha; hence the Japanese name.

三味線草

　　二十日鼠の

　　　　ちんどん屋

しゃみせんぐさ

　　はつかねずみの

　　　　ちんどんや

季語　三味線草(しゃみせんぐさ、ぺんぺん草、ペンペン

グサ、ナズナ、春)

ナズナは、「春の七草」の一つ。

Shamisen gusa

hatsuka nezumi no

chindon ya

The shepherd's purse

the street sandwich-man band mice

are playing three-string instruments

Season word: *shamisen gusa* (*nazuna*, shepherd's purse,

capsella bursa-pastoris; spring)

Nazuna is one of the "seven plants of spring."

蕗の薹

　　誰も知らずに

　　　　食べられず

ふきのとう

　　だれもしらずに

　　　　たべられず

季語　　蕗の薹（フキノトウ、春）

米国では、蕗の薹を食べる習慣はなく、鑑賞用に庭に育
てられている。

Fuki no tō

dare mo shirazu ni

taberarezu

Giant butterbur

no one knows about it

and no one eats it

Season word: *fuki no tō* (giant butterbur, *petasites japonicus*; spring)

Giant butterbur is an edible plant and is considered a delicacy of the spring in Japan, but it is grown as an ornamental plant in the United States and is not consumed.

南高梅

　　紀州の犬の

　　　　墓守る

なんこうばい

　　きしゅうのいぬの

　　　　はかまもる

季語　南高梅（ナンコウバイ、春）

2018年5月に和歌山県田辺市で怪死した「紀州のドンファ

ン」の愛犬は、検死解剖では毒殺ではないと判断されたが、

殺された可能性は拭い切れない。

Nankōbai

    Kishū no inu no

        haka mamoru

The Nankōbai plum blossoms

    guard

        the grave of the dog in Kishū

Season word: *Nankōbai* (*nankōbai* plum blossoms; spring)

Nankōbai is a species of plum cultivated in the Kishū

region (current Wakayama prefecture). On May 24, 2018,

a rich man in Tanabe, Wakayama prefecture, who was

referred to as the Don Juan of Kishū, died mysteriously and

his dog also died suddenly on May 6. The cause of his

death, possibly including murder, is under investigation.

幣辛夷

　　心の奥の

　　　　襞の綻ぶ

しでこぶし

　　こころのおくの

　　　　ひだのほころぶ

季語　幣辛夷（シデコブシ、春）

シデコブシは、20枚から30枚の花びらをつける。

Shide kobuhi

    kokoro no oku no

        hida no hokorobu

The star magnolia

    opens up

        the core of the soul in its many layers

Season word: *shide kobushi* (double-petalled magnolia,

star magnolia, *magnolia stellata*; spring)

Star magnolia has many petals, as many as twenty to thirty.

March

Photograph 3. Forget-me-not in the rain

黄水仙

　　望郷の丘

　　　　光る波

きずいせん

　　ぼうきょうのおか

　　　　ひかるなみ

季語　黄水仙（キズイセン、春）

Ki zuisen

    bōkyō no oka

        hikaru nami

The yellow daffodils bloom on the hill

    where one longs for one's hometown

        in the shining waves

Season word: *ki zuisen* (yellow daffodils; spring)

福島や

　　ぺんぺん草も

　　　　生えぬ丘

ふくしまや

　　ぺんぺんぐさも

　　　　はえぬおか

季語　ぺんぺん草（ペンペングサ、ナズナ、春）

ナズナは、「春の七草」の一つ。

Fukushima ya

penpen gusa mo

haenu oka

On the hill in Fukushima

even weeds like shepherd's purse

do not grow

Season word: *penpen gusa* (*nazuna*, shepherd's purse,

capsella bursa-pastoris; spring)

Nazuna is one of the "seven plants of spring." The soil in

Fukushima is still contaminated.

風信子

　　甘き香りを

　　　　福島へ

ひやしんす

　　あまきかおりを

　　　　ふくしまへ

季語　風信子（ヒヤシンス、春）

Hiyashinsu

amaki kaori o

Fukushima e

The hyacinth

sends forth its sweet fragrance

to Fukushima

Season word: *hiyashinsu* (hyacinth; spring)

蒲公英や

　　廃れし庭の

　　　　片隅に

たんぽぽや

　　すたれしにわの

　　　　かたすみに

季語　蒲公英（タンポポ、春）

Tanpopo ya

sutareshi niwa no

kata sumi ni

The dandelion blooms

at the corner

of the abandoned garden

Season word: *tanpopo* (dandelion; spring)

In Fukushima, most of the former residents have not been

able to go back to their houses.

黄水仙

　　廃校式の

　　　　送辞読む

きずいせん

　　はいこうしきの

　　　　そうじよむ

季語　黄水仙（キズイセン、春）

Ki zuisen

   haikō shiki no

      sōji yomu

The yellow daffodil

   reads the farewell address

      at the closing ceremony

         of the abolished public school

Season word: *ki zuisen* (yellow daffodil; spring)

In Fukushima and other rural areas in Japan, many public

schools have been abolished due to the shortage of

children.

すみれ草

　　タカラジェンヌの

　　　夢の道

すみれそう

　　タカラジェンヌの

　　　ゆめのみち

季語　すみれ草（スミレソウ、春）

阪急鉄道の兵庫県宝塚駅から宝塚劇場までの道は、「花

の道」と呼ばれる。

Sumiresō

　　Takarajen'nu no

　　　　yume no michi

The violets bloom

　　on the dream road

　　　　of the Takarazienne

Season word: *sumiresō* (violet; spring)

Takarazienne refer to the performers in the famed

Takarazuka Revue in Hyōgo prefecture and the violets

symbolizes its starlets. The Flower Road runs from the

Hankyū Railways' Takarazuka Station to the Takarazuka

Theater.

ブラームス

　　勿忘草に

　　　　託す愛

ブラームス

　　わすれなぐさに

　　　　たくすあい

季語　勿忘草（ワスレナグサ、春）

ヨハネス・ブラームス（1833 年−1897 年）とクララ・シューマ

ン（1819 年−1896 年）の親交は、長い間研究の対象とされ

てきた。

Burāmusu

wasure nagusa ni

takusu ai

Brahms

the young composer is entrusting his love

to the forget-me-not

Season word: *wasure nagusa* (forget-me-not; spring)

The platonic relationship between Johannes Brahms (1833–

1897) and Clara Schumann (1819–1896) has been much

studied.

三色菫

　　天使の吐息

　　　　風の聴く

さんしきすみれ

　　てんしのといき

　　　　かぜのきく

季語　　三色菫（サンシキスミレ、春）

Sanshiki sumire

tenshi no toiki

kaze no kiku

The tricolor violet

the wind is listening

to the sighs of the angel

Season word: *sanshiki sumire* (tricolor violet; spring)

華鬘草

　　届かぬ想ひ

　　　断ち切らん

けまんそう

　　とどかぬおもい

　　　たちきらん

季語　華鬘草（ケマンソウ、春）

ケマンソウは、ハート型のピンクの花を春につける。

Kemansō

todokanu omoi

tachi kiran

The bleeding heart blossoms

vow to give up

the unrequited love

Season word: *kemansō* (Asian bleeding-heart blossoms,

lamprocapnos spectabilis; spring)

京椿

　　茶筅の先を

　　　　吟味せり

きょうつばき

　　ちゃせんのさきを

　　　　ぎんみせり

季語　　京椿（京ツバキ、春）

千利休（1522 年−1591 年）は、椿を好んで茶席に活けた。

表千家は利休忌（旧暦 2 月 28 日）を毎年、3 月 27 日に、

裏千家は 3 月 28 日に行う。

Kyō tsubaki

chasen no saki o

ginmi seri

The Kyoto camellia

is examining intently

the tips of the bamboo tea whisk

Season word: *Kyō tsubaki* (Kyoto camellia; spring)

The Kyoto camellia is used for decoration at the tea

ceremony for the memorial anniversary day of Sen no

Rikyū (1522–1591). The Omote Senke school conducts

this memorial ceremony on March 27 while the Ura Senke

school conducts on March 28.

April

Photograph 4. Bonsai of Asahi 'mountain cherry'

blossoms (Asahi yama-zakura, *cerasus jamasakura*),

courtesy of © Watanabe Miyuki

富士桜

　　　樹海に眠る

　　　　　霊起こす

ふじざくら

　　　じゅかいにねむる

　　　　　れいおこす

季語　　富士桜（フジザクラ、春）

フジザクラは、別名、マメザクラという、早咲きの桜である。

Fuji zakura

jukai ni nemuru

rei okosu

Fuji cherry blossoms

have awakened the souls of the dead

in the Sea of Trees

Season word: *Fuji zakura* (*mame zakura*, Fuji cherry

blossoms; spring)

Fuji zakura is an early bloomer and bears small white

blossoms. The "Sea of Trees" refers to Aokigahara at the

foot of Mt. Fuji, which is known as the home of ghosts in

Japanese mythology and as a place for committing suicide.

風に乗る

　　自転車二台

　　　　土筆待つ

かぜにのる

　　じてんしゃにだい

　　　　つくしまつ

季語　　土筆（ツクシ、春）

Kaze ni noru

jitensha ni dai

tsukushi matsu

Riding on the wind

two bicycles are running

to the riverbank where horsetail shoots await

Season word: *tsukushi* (horsetail shoot; spring)

阿亀桜

　　英国の名付け

　　　　親に問ふ

おかめざくら

　　えいこくのなづけ

　　　　おやにとう

季語　阿亀桜（オカメザクラ、春）

オカメザクラは、イギリスのコリングウッド・イングラム（1880 年
−1981 年）が、ヒカンザクラとマメザクラを交配して作った早咲き
桜。阿亀の頬の色から連想しての命名かも知れないが、阿亀の
イメージとは全く異なる。オカメのことを美しい女性（あるいは、
「おとめ」）と誤解したのではないかとも思われる。一方、京都の
大報恩寺の「阿亀桜」はシダレザクラで、別品種である。

Okame zakura

Eikoku no nazuke

oya ni tou

The Okame cherry blossom

asks a question

to her godfather in England

Season word: *Okame zakura* (okame cherry blossoms, an early bloomer; spring)

The Okame cherry tree is a hybrid of *hikan zakura* and *mame zakura* created by the British plant collector, Collingwood "Cherry" Ingram (1880–1981). "Okame" refers to a mask in the shape of a female with plump cheeks and hence an ugly woman. In turn, this cherry tree has dainty pink flowers that bloom with faces down (like a maiden), and Okame seems to be a misnomer.

そよ風や

　　桜トンネル

　　　そっと過ぎ

そよかぜや

　　さくらトンネル

　　　そっとすぎ

季語　桜トンネル（さくらトンネル、春）

Soyo kaze ya

    sakura ton'neru

       sotto sugi

The breeze

    passes through the 'cherry blossom tunnel'

      gently and quietly

Season word: *sakura ton'neru* (*lit.*, "cherry blossom

tunnel"; spring)

A row of cherry trees on a street looks like a tunnel of

cherry blossoms.

姥桜

　　見守る伊予の

　　　　海と空

うばざくら

　　みまもるいよの

　　　　うみとそら

季語　　姥桜（うばざくら、エドヒガンザクラの一種、春）

愛媛県松山市にある国宝、大宝寺の姥桜伝説。乳母が自分の

命と引き替えに、るり姫の病気平癒を大宝寺の薬師に祈ったと

ころ、姫は治癒した。乳母は約束を守って、薬も飲まずに死ぬ。

以後、乳母の命日に、母乳のような色の桜が咲くという言い伝え。

ラフカディオ・ハーン（小泉八雲）の『怪談』に収められる。

Uba zakura

mimamoru Iyo no

umi to sora

The Nanny Cherry Tree

is watching over

the sea and the sky of Iyo

Season word: *Uba zakura* (*lit.*, "Nanny Cherry Tree," a

species of *Edo higan zakura*, an early bloomer; spring)

This 400-year old cherry tree stands at Taihō Temple (a National

Treasure of Japan) in Matsuyama, Ehime prefecture. The legend

has it that a nanny prayed to the temple for the sick princess, in

exchange for her own life. The princess healed and the nanny

died. Since then, the white sakura (milk color) has bloomed on

the nanny's memorial anniversary day every year to this day.

小糠雨

　　しっとり濡れる

　　　　花と娘と

こぬかあめ

　　しっとりぬれる

　　　　はなとこと

季語　　花（はな、春）

俳句では、「花」は桜のことを意味する。

Konuka ame

    shittori nureru

        hana to ko to

The drizzle is making

    the cherry blossoms and the girl

        wet gently

Season word: *konuka ame* (drizzle; spring)

In haiku, *hana* (flower) refers to cherry blossoms.

花冷えや

　　コロナの禍根

　　　　いよ深く

はなびえや

　　コロナのかこん

　　　　いよふかく

季語　花冷え（はなびえ、春）

「コロナ」は、2020 年春に猛威を振るった、新型コロ

ナ・ウイルスによる前代未聞の世界規模感染を指す。

Hana bie ya

Korona no kakon

iyo fukaku

The cold spell in the cherry blossom season

is making the Covid-19 pandemic

even worse

Season word: *hana bie* (a cold weather spell in the cherry

blossom season; spring)

桜散る

　　ランドセル無き

　　　校庭に

さくらちる

　　ランドセルなき

　　　こうていに

季語　桜散る（さくらちる、春）

Sakura chiru

randoseru naki

kōtei ni

The cherry blossoms are falling

on the school playground

where there are no children

Season word: *sakura chiru* (falling cherry blossoms;

spring)

コロナ冷え

　　花の魂

　　　　つゆと消え

コロナびえ

　　はなのたましい

　　　　つゆときえ

季語　花（はな、春）

「コロナ」は、2020 年春に猛威を振るった、新型コロ

ナ・ウイルスによる前代未聞の世界規模感染とその被

害を指す。俳句では、「花」は桜のことを意味する。

Korona bie

　　hana no tamashii

　　　　tsuyu to kie

In the cold spell in the cherry blossom season

　　during the Covid-19 pandemic

　　　　the soul of the cherry blossoms

　　　　　　has disappeared

Season word: *hana* (cherry blossoms; spring)

In haiku, *hana* (flower) refers to cherry blossoms.

花吹雪

　　コロナの死者を

　　　　埋めたり

はなふぶき

　　コロナのししゃを

　　　　うづめたり

季語　花吹雪（はなふぶき、春）

花吹雪は、桜吹雪のこと。「コロナ」は、2020 年春に猛威

を振るった、新型コロナ・ウイルスによる前代未聞の世

界規模感染を指す。

Hana fubuki

Korona no shisha o

uzume tari

The cherry blossom shower

is burying

the dead of the Covid-19 pandemic

Season word: *hana fubuki* (cherry blossom petal shower;

spring)

May

Photograph 5. Asian bleeding-heart blossoms (*kemansō*,

lamprocapnos spectabilis)

華鬘草

　　お対のペンダント

　　　　捨てる

けまんそう

　　おついのペンダント

　　　　すてる

季語　華鬘草（ケマンソウ、春）

ケマンソウは、ハート型のピンクの花を春につける。

Kemansō

o tsui no pendanto

suteru

The bleeding-heart blossoms

a young woman has thrown

her paired pendant away

Season word: *kemansō* (Asian bleeding-heart blossoms,

lamprocapnos spectabilis; spring)

コロナ禍や

　　　藤棚伐られ

　　　　堆く

コロナかや

　　　ふじだなきられ

　　　　うづたかく

季語　　藤棚（ふじだな、春）

コロナ感染防止策として、観光客を制限するため、断腸の

思いで藤の花を全て伐り落とした藤の名所。

Korona ka ya

    fuji dana kirare

        uzu takaku

The Covid-19 pandemic

    the wisteria on the terraces were all cut down

        and were piled on the ground

Season word: *fuji dana* (wisteria terrace; spring)

The caretakers at the famous wisteria garden cut down all

the wisteria blossoms from the terraces in order to

discourage tourists from flocking to see the gorgeous

flowers.

都忘れ

　　市女の笠の

　　　　落人見遣る

みやこわすれ

　　いちめのかさの

　　　　おちうどみやる

季語　都忘れ（ミヤコワスレ、春）

ミヤコワスレの別名は、野春菊（ノシュンギク）、東菊（アズマギク）

。白いベールのような薄い布が垂れ下がる市女笠は、平安時代

の中頃から上流貴族の女性が外出時に被るようになった。

Miyama wasure

ichime no kasa no

ochiudo miyaru

The purple aster is watching

the medieval noblewoman

wearing a travelling sedge hat

leave the capital

Season word: *miyako wasure* (*miyama yomena, gymnaster savalieri, aster savalieri*; spring)
This alludes to a scene in which a medieval noblewoman is moving to a remote region, whose husband was demoted at the court in Kyoto.

霞草

　　恥じらふ乙女

　　　　慈しむ

かすみそう

　　はじらうおとめ

　　　　いつくしむ

季語　　霞草（カスミソウ、春）

Kasumisō

hajirau otome

itsukushimu

The baby's breath

is embracing

the bashful maiden

Season word: *kasumisō* (baby's breath, *gypsophila*; spring)

花一華

　　　アドニスの死と

　　　　　ビーナスの愛

はないちげ

　　　アドニスのしと

　　　　　ビーナスのあい

季語　花一華（はないちげ、アネモネ、春）

ギリシア神話によると、アドニスの血がアネモネとなった。

Hana ichige

Adonisu no shi to

Viinasu no ai

The anemone witnessed

the death of Adonis

and the love of Venus

Season word: *hana ichige* (anemone, *anemone coronaria*;

spring)

In Greek mythology, the blood of Adonis became

anemones.

苧環や

　　ジョージ・フロイド

　　　悼む空

おだまきや

　　ジョージ・フロイド

　　　いたむそら

季語　苧環（オダマキ、春）

2020 年 5 月 25 日に、ミネソタ州ミネアポリスで、白人警官

が黒人のジョージ・フロイドを窒息死させた。

Odamaki ya

    Jōji Furoido

      itamu sora

The columbine mourns

    the death of George Floyd

      in the sky

Season word: *odamaki* (columbine; spring)

George Floyd was killed by a policeman in Minneapolis,

Minnesota, on May 25, 2020.

ブリーディング・ハート

民の怒りと

慟哭と

ブリーディング・ハート

たみのいかりと

どうこくと

季語　ブリーディング・ハート（華鬘草、ケマンソウ、春）

2020 年 5 月 25 日に、ミネソタ州ミネアポリスで、白人警官

が黒人のジョージ・フロイドを窒息死させたことに対して、

米国各地で抗議が沸き起こり、全世界に広まった。

Buriidingu hāto

tami no ikari to

dōkoku to

The bleeding-heart blossoms

embrace

the anger and grief of the people

Season word: *kemansō* (Asian bleeding-heart blossoms,

lamprocapnos spectabilis; spring)

The killing of George Floyd on May 25, 2020 caused

nationwide protests against racial injustice and

discrimination in the United States and other countries.

ニゲラ散る

　　ジョージ・フロイド

　　嘆き散る

ニゲラちる

　　ジョージ・フロイド

　　なげきちる

季語　ニゲラ（黒種草、クロタネソウ、夏）

ニゲラの語源は、黒を意味するラテン語、*niger*。

俳句では、5月5日から夏となる。

Nigera chiru

    Jōji Furoido

        nageki chiru

The nigella blossoms are falling

    they are falling

        grieving the death of George Floyd

Season word: *nigera* (nigella blossoms, *kurotanesō*, *lit.*, "blackseed plant"; summer)

'Nigella' derives from the Latin word *niger* (black). Its seedpods bear abundant black seeds; hence the Japanese name.

In haiku, May 5 marks the beginning of summer.

桐の花

　　吾子を慕ひて

　　　　芳しき

きりのはな

　　あこをしたいて

　　　　かぐわしき

季語　桐の花（キリのはな、夏）

Kiri no hana

    ako o shitai te

        kaguwa shiki

The princess tree blossoms

    send forth their fragrance to a woman

        reminiscing about her deceased daughter

Season word: *kiri no hana* (princess tree blossoms,

paulownia tomentosa; summer)

コーラ・ルイーズ

　　伊藤博士の

　　　　意志と汗

コーラ・ルイーズ

　　いとうはくしの

　　　　いしとあせ

季語　コーラ・ルイーズ（シャクヤクの一種、夏）

1948 年、園芸研究家の伊藤東一（とういち）博士は、シャ

クヤクとボタンを交配して、シャクヤクの品種改良に成功し

たが、新種の開花を見届けることなく死亡した。コーラ・ル

イーズは、「イトウ・ピオニー」の一種。

Kōra Ruiizu

Itō hakushi no

ishi to ase

The Cora Louise peonies

the will and the sweat

of Dr. Itoh

Season word: *Kōra Ruiizu* (Cora Louise, a species of

peonies; summer)

In 1948 in Japan, the horticulturist Dr. Toichi Itoh

succeeded in crossing herbaceous peonies with tree peonies

and produced peony hybrids; but died without seeing his

creations bloom. Cora Louise is one of the Itoh Peonies.

June

Photograph 6. Princess tree blossoms (*kiri no hana,*

paulownia tomentosa)

桐の花

　　吾子のたましひ

　　　甦り

きりのはな

　　あこのたましい

　　　よみがえり

季語　桐の花（キリのはな、夏）

Kiri no hana

   ako no tamashii

      yomi gaeri

The princess tree blossoms

   have resuscitated

      the soul of my dead daughter

Season word: *kiri no hana* (princess tree blossoms,

paulownia tomentosa; summer)

八橋や

　　待ち人来たり

　　　　燕子花

やつはしや

　　まちびときたり

　　　　かきつばた

季語　燕子花（カキツバタ、夏）

愛知県知立市八橋は、在原業平（825 年―880 年）が、『伊

勢物語』に有名な燕子花の短歌を書いたことで知られる。

Yatsu hashi ya

machi bito kitari

kaki tsubata

At Yatsu hashi

the iris had been waiting for the person

who finally came

Season word: *kaki tsubata* (Japanese iris; summer)

Yatsu hashi (*lit.*, "eight bridges") is the place in current

Chiryū, Aichi prefecture, where Ariwara no Narihira (825–

880) wrote the famous poem about the iris, which was

compiled into the *Ise monogatari* (The Tale of Ise).

ジュン・ブライド

　　純白のベールと

　　　　ジャスミンのブーケ

ジュン・ブライド

　　じゅんぱくのベールと

　　　　ジャスミンのブーケ

季語　ジャスミン（夏）

Jun buraido

junpaku no vēru

to jasumin no būke

The June bride is wearing

a pure white veil

and a jasmine bouquet

Season word: *jasumin* (jasmine; summer)

紫陽花や

　　ショパン奏でる

　　　　午後の雨

あじさいや

　　ショパンかなでる

　　　　ごごのあめ

季語　　紫陽花（アジサイ、夏）

フレデリック・ショパン（1818 年−1849 年）のプレリュード

Op. 28、No. 15、「雨だれの曲」より連想。

Ajisai ya

    Shopan kanaderu

        gogo no ame

The hydrangea

    is listening to the afternoon rain

        playing Chopin

Season word: *ajisai* (hydrangea; summer).

Chopin refers to the "Raindrop," Prelude, Op. 28, No. 15

by Frederic Chopin (1818–1849).

花菖蒲

　　紫式部の

　　　　筆と和紙

はなしょうぶ

　　むらさきしきぶの

　　　　ふでとわし

季語　花菖蒲（ハナショウブ、夏）

紫式部（970 年/978 年−1019 年?）は、『源氏物語』の著

者。

Hana shōbu

Murasaki Shikibu no

fude to washi

The Japanese irises

are observing

the traditional pen and paper

of Lady Shikibu

Season word: *hana shōbu* (Japanese iris; summer)

Lady Shikibu (between 970 and 978–1019?) is the author

of *The Tale of Genji*.

菖蒲咲く

　　斎王祭の

　　　　沿道に

しょうぶさく

　　さいおうまつりの

　　　　えんどうに

季語　菖蒲（ショウブ、夏）

斎王は、天皇に代わって伊勢神宮に仕えた皇族の女性の
こと。平安時代に十二単を纏った斎王が京都から伊勢ま
で向かった大行列のことを「斎王群行」と呼ぶ。斎宮跡の
ある三重県多気郡明和町の町の花は、野花菖蒲（ノハナ
ショウブ）で、町のシンボルカラーは紫色。

Shōbu saku

Saiō matsuri no

endō ni

The Japanese irises

welcome the procession

of the Princess Saiō Festival on the road

Season word: *shōbu* (Japanese iris; summer)

The Princess Saiō Festival is held in Meiwa, Mie

prefecture, in June, in honor of the "Imperial princess" who

used to serve at Ise Grand Shrine on behalf of emperors

during the Heian period. The princess' grand procession

walked on the road to Ise Grand Shrine from Kyoto.

桐の花

　　母の形見の

　　　　桐箪笥

きりのはな

　　ははのかたみの

　　　　きりだんす

季語　桐の花（キリのはな、夏）

Kiri no hana

    haha no katami no

        kiri dansu

The empress tree blossoms

    the daughter touches her mother's remembrance

        the kimono dresser

            made from the empress tree

Season word: *kiri no hana* (empress tree blossoms,

paulownia tomentosa; summer)

コロナ死者

　　花びらの散る

　　　　薔薇の園

コロナししゃ

　　はなびらのちる

　　　　ばらのその

季語　　薔薇（バラ、夏）

「コロナ」は、2020 年春に猛威を振るった、新型コロ

ナ・ウイルスによる前代未聞の世界規模感染とその被

害を指す。

Korona shisha

hana bira no chiru

bara no sono

The rose petals are falling

on the dead of the Covid-19 pandemic

in the rose garden

Season word: *bara* (rose; summer)

紫陽花や

　　　空の涙の

　　　　　色となり

あじさいや

　　　そらのなみだの

　　　　　いろとなり

季語　紫陽花（アジサイ、夏）

Ajisai ya

    sora no namida no

        iro to nari

The hydrangea

    has turned its color

        to that of the tears of the sky

Season word: *ajisai* (hydrangea; summer)

「ご自由に」

　　あやめの子株

　　　　門前に

「ごじゆうに」

　　あやめのこかぶ

　　　　もんぜんに

季語　あやめ（アヤメ、夏）

アヤメの株分け用に、切り分けた株が、「ご自由に」という

貼り紙と共に、家の前に置かれていたという実話。

"Gojiyū ni"

   ayame no ko kabu

    monzen ni

"Please take as you wish"

   the little note and divided iris rootstalks

    in front of the house

Season word: *ayame* (Japanese iris; summer)

Someone put out divided iris rootstalks (rhizomes) in front

of the house, along with a note, so that other people can

propagate the iris for free.

July

Photograph 7. Japanese honeysuckle (*suikazura, nindō,*

lonicera japonica)

忍冬の花

　　シェイクスピアの

　　　　夜の夢

にんどうのはな

　　シェイクスピアの

　　　　よるのゆめ

季語　忍冬の花（ニンドウのはな、スイカズラ、夏）

ウイリアム・シェイクスピア（1564 年—1616 年）の戯曲、『真

夏の夜の夢』には、スイカズラが随所に言及されている。

Nindō no hana

Shēkusupia no

yoru no yume

The Japanese honeysuckle

is reciting the Midsummer Night's Dream

of Shakespeare

Season word: *nindō no hana* (Japanese honeysuckle

blossoms, *suikazura, lonicera japonica*; summer)

The Japanese honeysuckle blossoms appear in *A

Midsummer Night's Dream* by William Shakespeare

(1564–1616), used as a canopy over Queen Tatiana and

elsewhere.

半夏生

　　青く真白く

　　　　雨降らす

はんげしょう

　　あおくましろく

　　　　あめふらす

季語　半夏生（ハンゲショウ、夏）

ハンゲショウは、別名、片白草（カタシロクサ）という。

暦の上では、半夏生は、夏至から数えて 11 日目のことを

指し、現在は、7 月 2 日頃にあたる。

Hangeshō

> aoku mashiroku
>
> ame furasu

The Asian lizard's tail

> it rains partly blue
>
> partly white

Season word: *hangeshō* (Asian lizard's tail, *saururus chinensis*; summer)

The Asian lizard's tail has partly green and partly white leaves, as if it wears makeup partially.

In the Japanese calendar, *hangeshō* refers to the 11th day after the summer solstice, which falls around July 2 today.

紅蓮や

　　平等院の

　　　　巫女となり

べにはすや

　　びょうどういんの

　　　　みことなり

季語　紅蓮（ベニハス、夏）

Beni hasu ya

    Byōdō in no

        miko to nari

The pink lotus flower

    has become the maiden

        of the Byōdō-in Temple

Season word: *beni hasu* (pink lotus flower; summer)

The Byōdō-in Temple in Uji, Kyoto prefecture, houses

many National Treasures of Japan.

夕顔や

　　徳川園に

　　　　眠る絵巻

ゆうがおや

　　とくがわえんに

　　　　ねるえまき

季語　　夕顔（ユウガオ、夏）

愛知県名古屋市の徳川園にある徳川美術館には、源氏
物語絵巻などの国宝が保存されている。「夕顔」は、『源氏
物語』の 54 帖の巻の一つ。

Yūgao ya

Tokugawa en ni

neru emaki

The evening primrose

the famed Picture Scrolls

lie in the Tokugawa Garden

Season word: *yūgao* (*lit*., "evening face," evening

primrose, bottle gourd; summer)

The Tokugawa Art Museum in the Tokugawa Garden in

Nagoya, Aichi prefecture, preserve the Picture Scrolls of

The Tale of Genji and other National Treasures of ancient

and medieval times.

立葵

　　光源氏の

　　　　忍び足

たちあおい

　　ひかるげんじの

　　　　しのびあし

季語　立葵（タチアオイ、夏）

Tachi aoi

   Hikaru Genji no

      shinobi ashi

The hollyhock

   watches the Shining Genji

      sneaking into the woman's house

Season word: *tachi aoi* (hollyhock; summer)

The Shining Genji is the protagonist in *The Tale of Genji.*

橘や

　　蹴鞠の遊ぶ

　　　　紫宸殿

たちばなや

　　けまりのあそぶ

　　　　ししんでん

季語　橘(タチバナ、夏)

Tachibana ya

kemari no asobu

Shishin den

The mandarin orange blossoms

the traditional kemari ball

is kicking at the Shishin Palace

Season word: *tachibana no hana* (mandarin orange

blossoms; summer).

Shishin Palace is the largest building in the Inner Palace of

the Heian Imperial Palace in Kyoto.

諏訪の湖

　　蓮華躑躅と

　　　　富士の山

すわのうみ

　　れんげつつじと

　　　　ふじのやま

季語　蓮華躑躅（レンゲツツジ、夏）

長野県塩尻市郊外の高ボッチ高原では、夏、朱色のレン

ゲツツジが山肌一帯を彩る。高原からは、諏訪湖、冠雪の

富士山や雄大な北アルプスが一望できる。

Suwa no umi

renge tsutsuji to

Fuji no yama

Lake Suwa

the Japanese azalea

looks at Mt. Fuji in the distance

Season word: *renge tsutsuji* (Japanese azalea,

rhododendron mole subsp. *japonicum*; summer)

The Takabotchi Highland in Shiojiri, Nagano prefecture, is

filled with the vermillion blossoms of the Japanese azalea

and one can overlook Lake Suwa and view the three tallest

mountains in Japan, including Mt. Fuji.

ラベンダー

　　富良野の里の

　　　　風の囁き

ラベンダー

　　ふらののさとの

　　　　かぜのささやき

季語　ラベンダー（夏）

Lavendā

Furano no sato no

kaze no sasayaki

The lavender

the wind is whispering

in the fields of Furano

Season word: *lavendā* (lavender; summer)

Furano, Hokkaidō, is famous for the lavender fields.

矢車菊

　　「青い眼」を乞ふ

　　　娘の涙

やぐるまぎく

　　「あおいめ」をこう

　　　このなみだ

季語　　矢車菊（ヤグルマギク、夏）

『青い眼が欲しい』（1970年）で知られる、トニ・モリソン

（1931年2月－2019年8月）は、ノーベル文学賞作家である。

Yaguruma giku

   aoi me o kou

      ko no namida

The cornflower

   the girl begs for the blue eyes

      and sheds tears

Season word: *yaguruma giku* (cornflower; summer)

This refers to *The Bluest Eyes* (1970) by the Nobel

Literature Prize laureate Toni Morrison (February 1931–

August 2019).

酢漿や

　　道化師トランプの

　　　　クラブ

かたばみや

　　どうけしトランプの

　　　　クラブ

季語　酢漿（カタバミ、夏）

カタバミの葉は、トランプ・カードのクラブに似ている。

Kata bami ya

dōkeshi Toranpu

no kurabu

The creeping wood sorrel

sneers at the club card

of Clown Trump

Season word: *kata bami* (creeping wood sorrel, *oxalis*

corniculata; summer)

The creeping wood sorrel leaves look like the club of trump

cards.

ベルサイユ

　　紅薔薇の散る

　　　　ギロチン台

ベルサイユ

　　べにばらのちる

　　　　ギロチンだい

季語　紅薔薇（べにばら、夏）

Verusaiyu

beni bara no chiru

girochin dai

The rose at the Versailles Palace

remembers the red rose petals

falling on the guillotine stand

Season word: *beni bara* (red rose; summer)

茉莉花や

　　故国懐かし

　　　　アラビアの

まつりかや

　　ここくなつかし

　　　　アラビアの

季語　茉莉花（マツリカ、アラビアン・ジャスミン、夏）

Matsurika ya

kokoku natsukashi

Arabia no

The jasmine

misses its homeland

in Arabia far away

Season word: *matsurika* (Arabian jasmine; summer)

薔薇の香に

　　包まれ眠る

　　　　オーロラ姫

ばらのかに

　　つつまれねむる

　　　　オーロラひめ

季語　薔薇（バラ、夏）

シャルル・ペロー（1628 年−1703 年）の童話、『眠れる森の

美女』に寄せて。

Bara no ka ni

tsutsu mare nemuru

Ōrora hime

Princess Aurora sleeps

being filled

with the fragrance of roses

Season word: *bara* (rose; summer)

Princess Aurora is the protagonist in the classic fairy tale,

The Sleeping Beauty by Charles Perrault (1628–1703).

月明り

　　プールに泳ぐ

　　　　ガーディニア

つきあかり

　　プールにおよぐ

　　　　ガーディニア

季語　ガーディニア（梔子、クチナシ、夏）

Tsuki akari

   pūru ni oyoku

      gādinia

In the moonlight

   the gardenias are floating

      in the swimming pool

Season word: *gādinia* (common gardenia; summer)

「薔薇のアダージョ」

　　眠れる森の

　　　覚めたり

「ばらのアダージョ」

　　ねむれるもりの

　　　めざめたり

季語　薔薇（バラ、夏）

チャイコフスキー（1840 年–1893 年）作曲のバレエ組曲、

『眠れる森の美女』Op. 66（1889 年）の「ローズ・アダージョ」

は、第一幕の見せ場である。

Bara no adājo

nemureru mori no

mezame tari

The Rose Adagio

the forest is awakening

to the tune

Season word: *bara* (rose; summer)

The Rose Adagio refers to the "Grand adage à la rose" of

The Sleeping Beauty, Op. 66 (1889), the ballet music

composed by Pyotr Ilyich Tchaikovsky (1840–1893).

August

Summer camellia (*natsu tsubaki*, *shara no ki*, Japanese stewartia), courtesy of © Watanabe Miyuki

夏椿

　　墓に寄り添ひ

　　　風の止む

なつつばき

　　はかによりそい

　　　かぜのやむ

季語　夏椿（ナツツバキ、沙羅の木、シャラノキ、夏）

夏椿は、朝に開花し、夕方に落花する、一日花である。

インドの聖木、沙羅双樹の代わりとして、日本の寺院に植

えられている。

Natsu tsubaki

haka ni yorisoi

kaze no yamu

The Japanese summer camellia

keeps company with the grave

and the wind stops

Season word: *natsu tsubaki* (*lit.*, "summer camellia," *shara no ki*, Japanese stewartia; summer)

The flower of this medium-sized deciduous tree native to Japan blooms only for a day. The tree is also called *shara no ki*, because it looks similar to the sal tree, the sacred tree in India. The summer camellia adorns many Buddhist temples in Japan, as a substitute for the sal tree.

泰山木

　　白き香に酔ふ

　　　　夏の月

たいさんぼく

　　しろきかによう

　　　　なつのつき

季語　泰山木の花（タイサンボクのはな、夏）　夏の月（な

つのつき、夏）

Taisanboku

shiroki ka ni you

natsu no tsuki

The southern magnolia

the summer moon is intoxicated

by its white fragrance

Season words: *taisanboku no hana* (southern magnolia

blossoms, *Magnolia grandiflora*; summer) and *natsu no*

tsuki (summer moon; summer)

大賀蓮

　　太古の悟り

　　　　開く朝

おおがはす

　　たいこのさとり

　　　　ひらくあさ

季語　　大賀蓮（オオガハス、夏）

1951 年 3 月―4 月、千葉県検見川の遺跡から二千年前の

古代ハスの種 3 粒が発堀された。翌年 7 月、植物学者、

大賀一郎（1883 年―1964 年）のチームが、1 粒の種の発

芽・開花に成功し、オオガハスと名付けられた。

Ōga hasu

taiko no satori

hiraku asa

The Ōga lotus

has awakened the ancient enlightenment

in the morning

Season word: *hasu* (lotus; summer)

In March–April 1951, three seeds of a lotus of two

thousands years ago were excavated in the ancient ruins in

Kemigawa, Chiba prefecture. The botanist, Dr. Ōga Ichirō

(1883–1964), succeeded in making one of the seeds

germinate and bloom in July 1952; hence the Ōga lotus.

玫瑰や

　　　御座白浜の

　　　　　山と空

はまなすや

　　　ござしらはまの

　　　　　やまとそら

季語　玫瑰(ハマナス、夏)

御座白浜は、三重県志摩の御座半島の岬近くにある美し

い海辺。

Hama nasu ya

   Goza Shira hama no

      yama to sora

The beach roses

   at Goza Shirahama

      watch the mountains and the sky

Season word: *hama nasu* (beach rose, *rosa rugosa*; summer)

Goza Shirahama is a pristine beach at the tip of the Goza peninsula in Shima, Mie prefecture.

泰山木

　　「大三角」を

　　　　仰ぎ見る

たいさんぼく

　　だいさんかくを

　　　　あおぎみる

季語　泰山木の花（タイサンボクのはな、夏）

「大三角」は、琴座のベガ、白鳥座のデネブ、鷲座のアル

タイルの描く三角形のこと。

Taisanboku

　　Daisankaku o

　　　aogi miru

The southern magnolia

　　is admiring the Triangle

　　　in the night sky

Season word: *taisanboku no hana* (southern magnolia

blossoms, *Magnolia grandiflora*; summer)

The Triangle refers to the configuration of the

constellations Lyra the Harp (Vega being its alpha star),

Cygnus the Swan (Deneb), and Aquila the Eagle (Altair).

古代蓮

　　義経の霊

　　　　蘇る

こだいはす

　　よしつねのれい

　　　　よみがえる

季語　古代蓮（コダイハス、夏）

1950 年、岩手県平泉町にある中尊寺で、源義経（1159 年
−1189 年）を匿った藤原泰衡（1155 年−1189 年）の首桶から百
粒の古代ハスが発見された。1998 年、大賀一郎博士の門弟が
発芽・開花に成功し、「中尊寺ハス」（泰衡ハス）と命名された。

Kodai hasu

　　Yoshitsune no rei

　　　yomi gaeru

The ancient lotus

　　has resuscitated the spirit

　　　of Minamoto no Yoshitsune

Season word: *hasu* (lotus; summer)

Seeds of an ancient lotus were found in 1950 in the head canister

of Fujiwara no Yasuhira (1155–1189) in Chūson Temple in

Hiraizumi, Iwate prefecture, who had provided refuge for

Minamoto no Yoshitsune (1159–1189) in exile by his brother

Minamoto no Yoritomo (1147–1199). The seeds germinated and

bloomed in 1998; hence, the Chūsonji hasu (the Yasuhira lotus).

名古屋城

　　堀の紅蓮

　　　　いづこなり

なごやじょう

　　ほりのべにはす

　　　　いずこなり

季語　　紅蓮（ベニハス、夏）

愛知県名古屋市の名古屋城の外堀に毎夏咲いていた紅

蓮が消えた。外来種のアリゲータガー（肉食）が堀の生態

系を荒らしたという説もあるが、真相は解明されていない。

Nagoya jō

    hori no beni hasu

      izuko nari

Nagoya Castle

    where did the pink lotus blossoms

      in the outer moat go?

Season word: *beni hasu* (pink lotus; summer)

The gorgeous pink lotus blossoms used to fill the outer moat of

Nagoya Castle; but they all disappeared. One of the possible

causes is said to be the alligator gar (designated as an invasive

alien species) that made the moat its home. Although

carnivorous, it might have destroyed the habitat.

凌霄葛

　　帰米の朝の

　　　　写真撮影

のうぜんかずら

　　きべいのあさの

　　　　しゃしんさつえい

季語　凌霄葛（ノウゼンカズラ、夏）

蔓（つる）性のノウゼンカズラは、鮮やかなオレンジ色の花

を夏空に咲かせる。

Nōzen kazura

kibei no asa no

shashin satsuei

The Chinese trumpet vine

watches a picture being taken

on the morning of leaving home

to go back to the United States

Season word: *nōzen kazura* (Chinese trumpet vine;

summer)

蓮の葉を

　　傘に道往く

　　　　放浪の画家

はすのはを

　　かさにみちゆく

　　　　ほうろうのがか

季語　蓮の葉（ハスのは、夏）

「放浪の画家」は、「日本のゴッホ」と言われた山下清

（1922 年—1971 年）。自伝『放浪日記』（1956 年）は、『裸

の大将放浪記』としてテレビドラマ化され、人気を博した。

Hasu no ha o

   kasa ni michi yuku

      hōrō no gaka

The wandering painter

   is walking on the road

      using the lotus leaf as an umbrella

Season word: *hasu no ha* (lotus leaf; summer)

The wandering painter refers to Yamashita Kiyoshi (1922–

1971), who was dubbed the Japanese van Gogh. He travelled

throughout Japan on foot, penniless, sleeping in the railroad

stations. He is most famous for his chigiri-e *(lit.,* paintings made

of hand-torn pieces of colored paper, like mosaic art).

荔枝の実

　　楊玉環の

　　　　栄枯盛衰

らいちのみ

　　ようぎょくかんの

　　　　えいこせいすい

季語　荔枝の実（ライチのみ、夏）

楊玉環（719 年—756 年）は、楊貴妃の実名。ライチの実が

好物であったといわれる。

Laichi no mi

   Yō Gyokukan no

      eiko seisui

The lychee fruit

   the rise and fall

      of Yang Yuhuan

Season word: *laichi no mi* (lychee fruit; summer)

Yang Yuhuan is the real name of Yang Guifei (719–756),

the Imperial consort of Tang dynasty emperor Xuanzong

(685–762). Lychee fruit was her favorite food.

蓮消えし

　　カリフォルニアの

　　　　失楽園

はすきえし

　　カリフォルニアの

　　　　しつらくえん

季語　　蓮（ハス、夏）

2008 年、カリフォルニア州ロサンジェルスにあるエコー・パークのベニハスがほとんど消えた。水質汚染が原因で、市当局は湖の修復プロジェクトに着手。2013 年、ハスの花が戻った。

Hasu kieshi

Kariforunia no

shitsuraku en

The lotus has disappeared

in the park in California

and it has become a Paradise Lost

Season word: *hasu* (lotus; summer)

The lotus blossoms in Echo Park in Los Angeles that had

been an icon of summer in the urban space almost

disappeared in 2008. The pollution in the lake had killed

the fish and the lotus. The city authorities undertook

habitat restoration. In 2013, the flowers came back.

夏の宵

　　月を待つかに

　　　　金糸梅

なつのよい

　　つきをまつかに

　　　　きんしばい

季語　夏の宵（なつのよい、夏）　金糸梅（キンシバイ、夏）

Natsu no yoi

tsuki o matsu kani

kinshibai

In the summer evening

the golden cup blooms

as if waiting for the moon

Season words: *natsu no yoi* (summer evening, summer) and *kinshibai* (golden cup, St. John's wort, yellow mosqueta, *hypericum patulum*; summer)

昼咲月見草

　　　風と光と

　　　　　戯れる

ひるざきつきみそう

　　　かぜとひかりと

　　　　　たわむれる

季語　昼咲月見草（ヒルザキ・ツキミソウ、メキシカン・プリ

ムローズ、夏）

メキシカン・プリムローズは、愛らしいピンクの花をつけるが、

繁殖力が強く、一度植えると、すぐに庭一杯に広がり、除

去することが困難である。

Hiruzaki tsukimisō

kaze to hikari to

tawamureru

The Mexican primroses

are frolicking

with the wind and the sunlight

Season word: *hiruzaki tsukimisō* (Mexican primrose, pink

ladies, *oenothera speciosa*; summer)

Although dainty and pretty, this plant is extremely invasive

and is hard to remove from a garden once it was planted.

待宵草

　　進駐軍の

　　　　家の跡

まつよいぐさ

　　しんちゅうぐんの

　　　　いえのあと

季語　待宵草（マツヨイグサ、夏）

マツヨイグサは、幕末に日本に渡来した南米原産の帰化植物。丈夫で山野や河原に自生する。黄色の四弁花は、夕暮れに咲き始め、明け方になると萎んで、オレンジ色になる。米軍日本占領終了後も、米人の住んでいた家の跡地に咲いていた。

Matsuyoi gusa

Shinchū gun no

ie no ato

The evening primrose blooms

in the house

where the American GI used to live

Season word: *matsuyoi gusa* (evening primrose, *oenothera stricta*; summer)

The evening primrose, native to South America, continued to grow at the American house, after the residents had gone home, who were stationed in Japan during the occupation of Japan. Its yellow flower blooms in the evening and turns orange in the morning.

月見草

　　探ね彷徨ふ

　　　宵と闇

つきみそう

　　たずねさまよう

　　　よいとやみ

季語　　月見草（ツキミソウ、夏）

ツキミソウは、幕末に日本に渡来した北米原産の植物。夕方に
四弁の白の清楚な花を咲かせ、明け方になると、萎んで淡紅色
になる。待宵草とよく混同されるが、マツヨイグサのように丈夫で
なく、野生化することなくほとんど見られなくなった「幻の花」。

Tsukimisō

    tazune samayou

        yoi to yami

One is wandering

    in the dark in the evening

        in search of the white evening primrose

Season word: *tsukimisō* (four-wing evening primrose,

oenothera tetraptera; summer)

In Japanese culture and literature, *tsukimisō* (four-wing

evening primrose) has been mistakenly used for *matsuyoi*

gusa (evening primrose). The former has white flowers

and is almost extinct in Japan today, whereas the latter has

yellow flowers and is invasive.

September

Photograph 9. Morning glory in the rain

朝顔や

　　日中友好の

　　　証し

あさがおや

　　にっちゅうゆうこうの

　　　あかし

季語　朝顔（アサガオ、秋）

愛新覚羅溥儀（1906 年−1967 年）の弟、溥傑（1907 年
−1994 年）に嫁いだ浩（旧姓嵯峨、1914 年−1987 年）は、
日本からアサガオの種を中国に持参し、文化大革命中、
周恩来首相の庇護下、北京で育てた。

Asagao ya

    Nitchū yūkō no

       akashi

The morning glory

    tied together

       the friendship between China and Japan

Season word: *asagao* (morning glory; autumn)

Lady Saga Hiro (1914–1987) married Pujie (1907–1994), the

younger brother of China's last emperor Puyi (1906–1967),

brought seeds of the morning glory to China, and grew them in

their hideout in Beijing while enduring persecution during the

Cultural Revolution, protected by Premier Zhou Enlai.

葛の花

　　内緒話を

　　　　聴かせたり

くずのはな

　　ないしょばなしを

　　　　きかせたり

季語　葛の花（クズの花、秋）

クズの花は、「秋の七草」の一つ。

Kuzu no hana

naisho banashi o

kikase tari

The arrowroot blossoms

are telling

a secret story

Season word: *kuzu no hana* (East Asian arrowroot

blossoms; autumn)

The East Asian arrowroot is one of the "seven plants of

autumn."

酔芙蓉

　　ときめく胸を

　　　　　なだめつつ

すいふよう

　　ときめくむねを

　　　　　なだめつつ

季語　酔芙蓉（スイフヨウ、秋）

スイフヨウは、午前中は白色であるが、午後にはピンク色

に変わる、一日花。

Sui fuyō

tokimeku mune o

nadame tsutsu

The drunken cotton rose mallow

is trying to calm down

the excited heart gradually

Season word: *sui fuyō* (*lit.*, "drunken cotton rose mallow,"

hibiscus mutabilis cv. *versicolor*; autumn)

This flower changes its color from white in the morning to

pink in the afternoon; hence the Japanese name, and

blooms only for a day.

花秋葵

　　誕生日待ち

　　　　咲きにけり

はなおくら

　　たんじょうびまち

　　　　さきにけり

季語　　花秋葵（ハナオクラ、トロロアオイ、秋）

ハナオクラは、ハイビスカスによく似た、美しいクリーム色

の花を咲かせる。

Hana okura

    tanjōbi machi

        sakini keri

The flowering okra

    has waited to blossom

        on one's birthday

Season word: *hana okura* (aibika, sunset musk mallow,

sunset hibiscus, *abelmoschus manihot*; autumn)

This plant has gorgeous lemon-yellow flowers that

resemble hibiscus.

秋明菊

　　未生流派の

　　　　師の鋏

しゅうめいぎく

　　みしょうりゅうはの

　　　　しのはさみ

季語　秋明菊（シュウメイギク、秋）

シュウメイギクは、その名前にも拘らず、アネモネの仲間で

あり、その花はアネモネによく似ている。未生流は、未生

斎一甫（みしょうさいいっぽ、1761 年−1824 年）を流祖とす

る華道の一派である。

Shūmei giku

Mishō ryū ha no

shi no hasami

The Japanese anemone

the Mishō School master

has a pair of scissors in his hand

Season word: *shūmei giku* (Japanese anemone, *anemone*

hupehensis; autumn)

Despite its Japanese name *shūmei giku* (*lit.,* "autumn bright

chrysanthemum"), it belongs to the genus of anemones.

The Mishō School is one of the traditional flower

arrangement schools.

蓮華の升麻

　　心の扉

　　　　開く風

れんげのしょうま

　　こころのとびら

　　　　ひらくかぜ

季語　蓮華の升麻（蓮華升麻、レンゲショウマ、秋）
アネモネに似た薄紫色の清楚で気品あふれる花は、「森
の妖精」と呼ばれる。東京都青梅市の御岳山（みたけさん）
などに群生する。その様子は、野山に咲くシュウメイギクの
ように見える。

Renge no shōma

    kokoro no tobira

        hiraku kaze

The 'Japanese mountain anemone'

    opens one's heart

        in the autumn breeze

Season word: *renge shōma* (*anemonopsis macrophylla*;

autumn)

This plant native to Japan has dainty purple flowers that

could be likened to a "Japanese mountain anemone."

花秋葵

　　恩送りの日

　　　　いよ来たり

はなおくら

　　おんおくりのひ

　　　　いよきたり

季語　花秋葵（ハナオクラ、トロロアオイ、秋）
野菜のオクラは、ハナオクラによく似た花を咲かせるが、そ
の花は、野菜の中で最も美しいといわれる。

Hana okura

    on okuri no hi

        iyo kitari

The flowering okra

    the day to repay one's indebtedness

        has finally come

Season word: *hana okura* (aibika, sunset musk mallow,

sunset hibiscus, *abelmoschus manihot*; autumn)

Okra, the vegetable, bears a similar flower to *hana okura*,

which is considered the most beautiful among the vegetable

flowers.

紅木槿

　　叶わぬ願ひ

　　　　無窮の空に

べにむくげ

　　かなわぬねがい

　　　　むきゅうのそらに

季語　　紅木槿（ベニムクゲ、秋）

Beni mukuge

kanawanu negai

mukyū no sora ni

The Rose of Sharon

thinks of the unattainable wish

in the endless sky

Season word: *beni mukuge* (common hibiscus, Rose of

Sharon, Korean rose, *hibiscus syriacus*; autumn)

秋海棠

　　人の心の

　　　　測りしれなさ

しゅうかいどう

　　ひとのこころの

　　　　はかりしれなさ

季語　秋海棠（シュウカイドウ、秋）

Shūkaidō

hito no kokoro no

hakari shirenasa

The hardy begonia laments

it is hard to fathom

other people's hearts

Season word: *shūkaidō* (hardy begonia, *begonia grandis*; autumn)

青桔梗

　　「明智の寺」に

　　　　忍び咲き

あおききょう

　　「あけちのてら」に

　　　　しのびざき

季語　　青桔梗（アオキキョウ、秋）

明智光秀（1516/1528 年−1582 年）の家紋は、「水色桔

梗」。京都府亀岡市にある古刹（こさつ）、谷性寺（こくし

ょうじ、別名は「光秀寺」）の境内には光秀の首塚と伝

わる石塔があり、毎年、キキョウが咲き乱れる。

Ao kikyō

　　Akechi no tera ni

　　　shinobi zaki

The blue balloon flowers

　　bloom quietly

　　　in the Temple of Akechi

Season word: *kikyō* (balloon flower, *platycodon
grandiflorus*; autumn)

Akechi Mitsuhide (1516/1528–1582) staged a coup d'état at the
Hon'nō Temple to assassinate Oda Nobunaga (1534–1582). His
head canister is buried at the Kokujō Temple in Kameoka, Kyoto
prefecture. His family crest is the design of the "water-color
balloon flower," which blooms in this temple every year.

October

Photograph 10. "October cherry blossoms" (*jūgatsu zakura*) against a background of fall foliage

十月桜

　　爺の柴犬

　　　　生き返る

じゅうがつざくら

　　じいのしばいぬ

　　　　いきかえる

季語　十月桜（ジュウガツザクラ、秋）

ジュウガツザクラは、4月と10月と、年2回開花する。八重咲

きの桜で、花は、淡い紅色で蕚筒（がくとう）は紅色。

Jūgatsu zakura

jii no Shiba inu

iki kaeru

The October cherry blossoms

have resuscitated

the Shiba inu of the old man

Season word: *jūgatsu zakura* (*lit.*, "October cherry blossoms"; autumn)

The species blossoms twice a year in April and October, whose pink flowers are double-petalled. This refers to the folktale in which the old man resuscitated the dead flowering cherry tree by scattering the ashes of the tree by which he had buried his dog killed by the mean neighbor.

白菊や

　　吾子の化身か

　　　　三回忌

しらぎくや

　　あこのけしんか

　　　　さんかいき

季語　　白菊（シラギク、秋）

Shira giku ya

    ako no keshin ka

        sankai ki

The white chrysanthemum

    a reincarnation of my daughter

        at the three-year memorial anniversary day

Season word: *shira giku* (white chrysanthemum; autumn)

秋の薔薇

　　　「花の数式」

　　　　　教えたり

あきのばら

　　　「はなのすうしき」

　　　　　おしえたり

季語　秋の薔薇（あきのバラ、秋）

「フィボナッチ数列」で知られる、イタリアの数学者、レオナ

ルド・フィボナッチ（1170 年頃－1240 年/1250 年）は、「花

の数式」（花びらの数の方式）を発見した。

Aki no bara

   "Hana no sūshiki"

      oshie tari

The autumn rose

   is teaching

      the "Flower Formula"

Season word: *aki no bara* (autumn rose; autumn)

Italian mathematician Leonardo Fibonacci (c.1170–c.

1240/1250) discovered the "Flower Formula" in which the

number of flower petals follows certain rules.

渡月橋

　　　倒れ紅葉の

　　　　　心裂く

とげつきょう

　　　たおれもみじの

　　　　　こころさく

季語　　紅葉（もみじ、秋）

2018年9月4日、台風21号の猛威により、京都嵐山の渡月

橋の欄干が100メートルに渡り、なぎ倒された。

Togetsu kyō

taore momiji no

kokoro saku

The Togetsu Bridge fell

and the heart of the fall foliage

was torn

Season word: *momiji* (fall foliage; autumn)

On September 4, 2018, a strong typhoon destroyed most of

the Togetsu Bridge, in Arashiyama, Kyoto prefecture,

which is one of the most famous maple fall foliage viewing

spots in Kyoto.

白萩や

　　緋袴の裾

　　　　回廊を

しらはぎや

　　ひばかまのすそ

　　　　かいろうを

季語　白萩（シラハギ、秋）

Shira hagi ya

    hi bakama no suso

        kairō o

The white Japanese clover

    the sound of the hems of the red hakamas

        travelling along the corridor

Season word: *shira hagi* (white Japanese clover, bush

clover, *lespedeza*; autumn)

The red hakama (traditional long skirts) were worn by

women in the Imperial court and by maidens who serve at

Shinto shrines.

金の水引

　　狐の婚礼

　　　　祝いかな

きんのみずひき

　　きつねのこんれい

　　　　いわいかな

季語　　金の水引（金水引、キンミズヒキ、秋）

キンミズヒキの花穂は、キツネの尻尾のように見える。

Kin no mizuhiki

    kitsune no konrei

        iwai kana

The golden mizuhiki

    is tying up the gifts

        for the fox wedding

Season word: *kin no mizuhiki* (*kin mizuhiki*, *lit.*, "golden

mizuhiki," *agrimonia pilosa* var. *japonica*; autumn)

This plant has a long spike with dainty golden flowers that

resemble "mizuhiki," decorative strings that are used to tie

gifts for formal occasions. The flower spike could also be

likened to a fox tail.

スプレー菊

　　娘の留守に

　　　　届けたり

スプレーぎく

　　むすめのるすに

　　　　とどけたり

季語　スプレー菊（スプレーギク、秋）

Supurei giku

musume no rusu ni

todote tari

The spray mums

the mother delivers them

to her daughter's house while she is away

Season word: *supurei giku* (spray mums; autumn)

柳散る

　　美登利と信如

　　　　逢ひし門

やなぎちる

　　みどりとしんにょ

　　　　あいしもん

季語　柳散る（やなぎちる、秋）

樋口一葉（1872年−1896年）の『たけくらべ』（1896年）は、

「回れば大門の見返り柳いと長けれど、、、」で始まる。

235

Yanagi chiru

Midori to Shin'nyo

aishi mon

The willow leaves are falling

where Midori and Shin'nyo

used to meet

Season word: *yanagi chiru* (falling willow leaves; autumn)

This refers to a story, *Take kurabe* (Growing up, 1896) by

Higuchi Ichiyō (1872–1896).

黄昏に

　　ガス燈灯す

　　　　八重の菊

たそがれに

　　ガスとうともす

　　　　やえのきく

季語　　八重の菊（八重菊、ヤエギク、秋）

Tasogare ni

gasu tō tomosu

yae no kiku

At sunset

the double-petalled chrysanthemums

light the gaslight

Season word: *yae no kiku* (*yae-giku*, double-petalled

chrysanthemum; autumn)

風そよぎ

　　　林檎の気持ち

　　　　揺らぎたり

かぜそよぎ

　　　りんごのきもち

　　　　ゆらぎたり

季語　　林檎（リンゴ、秋）

Kaze soyogi

   ringo no kimochi

     yuragi tari

The wind blows

   and sways

     the feelings of the apple

Season word: *ringo* (apple; autumn)

November

Photograph 11. American cranberry bush (highbush cranberry, *viburnum opulus var. americanum*)

檀弓の実

　　万葉の道

　　　　眩かり

まゆみのみ

　　まんようのみち

　　　　まばゆかり

季語　檀弓（マユミ、山錦木、ヤマニシキギ、秋）

万葉集に謳われたマユミは、よくしなるので古来より弓の材料と

して用いられた。初夏に薄緑色の小花をつけ、秋には紅葉と特

徴のある赤い実（熟すと割れて真っ赤な種子を４つ垂らす）が

美しい。奈良県の「山辺の道」には万葉集の歌碑が多く立つ。

Mayumi no mi

    Man'yō no michi

        mabayukari

The berries of the Himalayan spindle

    on the Man'yō Road

        are dazzling one's eyes

Season word: *mayumi no mi* (berries of Hamilton's spindle tree, Himalayan spindle, *euonymus hamiltonianus*; autumn) This tree bearing dainty, beautiful red berries in autumn was mentioned in Japan's oldest poem anthology, *Man'yō-shū*. The Manyō Road refers to Yamanobe no michi in Nara prefecture (the ancient capital), where many stone statues of poems compiled in *Man'yō-shū* adorn the street.

キャンパスの

　　蔦の葉の聴く

　　　　講義かな

キャンパスの

　　つたのはのきく

　　　　こうぎかな

季語　蔦（ツタ、秋）

Kyanpasu no

tsuta no ha no kiku

kōgi kana

The ivy leaves

on the campus

are listening to the lecture

Season word: *tsuta no ha* (ivy leaves; autumn)

七竈

　　　七人の子の

　　　　　　眼の光る

ななかまど

　　　ななにんのこの

　　　　　　めのひかる

季語　七竈（ナナカマド、秋）

ナナカマドの木は固く、その薪は、七度かまどに入れても

燃え残るほど丈夫であることからの命名。

Nana kamado

nana nin no ko no

me no hikaru

The Japanese rowan stove fire

the eyes of the seven children

light up

Season word: *nana kamado (lit.*, "seven-firewood stove,"
Japanese rowan, *sorbus commixta*; autumn)
This tree native to Japan is so sturdy that it is said to
withstand repeated use as firewood in the stove; hence the
Japanese name. The fall foliage and berries of this tree are
bright red.

山葡萄

　　　愉快な森の

　　　　　宴かな

やまぶどう

　　　ゆかいなもりの

　　　　　うたげかな

季語　山葡萄（ヤマブドウ、秋）

Yama budō

    yukai na mori no

       utage kana

The wild grapes

    a merry banquet

       in the forest

Season word: *yama budō* (wild grape; autumn)

ピラカンサ

　　万の嘴

　　　　燃やしたり

ピラカンサ

　　まんのくちばし

　　　　もやしたり

季語　ピラカンサ（常盤山楂の実、トキワサンザシのみ、

秋）

Pirakansa

man no kuchi bashi

moyashi tari

The firethorn berries

are burning

tens of thousands of beaks

Season word: *pirakansa* (firethorn, *pyracantha*; autumn)

December

Photograph 12. Christmas rose

冬薔薇

　　ルクセンブルクの

　　　非業の死

ふゆそうび

　　ルクセンブルクの

　　　ひごうのし

季語　冬薔薇（ふゆそうび、冬）

ポーランドに生まれ、ドイツに帰化した革命家ローザ・

ルクセンブルク（1871年−1919年）の友人への書簡は、

『獄中からの手紙』（1982年、2011年）として出版された。

弱者への同情と自然への共感に溢れる内容。

Fuyu sōbi

    Rukusenburuku no

       higō no shi

The winter rose wails

    over the tragic death

       of Rosa Luxemburg

Season word: *fuyu sōbi* (winter rose; winter)

Letters of the Polish/German revolutionary socialist Rosa

Luxemburg (1871–1919), written in prison to her childhood

friend, have been published as *Gokuchū kara no tegami*

(Letters from Prison, 1982, 2011), embracing her sympathy

to the weak, empathy to nature, and appreciation of culture.

忘れ花

　　路傍の石の

　　　　かたはらに

わすればな

　　ろぼうのいしの

　　　　かたわらに

季語　　忘れ花（わすればな、冬に咲く時ならぬ花、冬）

山本有三（1887 年−1974 年）の代表作、『路傍の石』

（1937 年−1940 年）は、検閲などの影響により断筆され、

未完に終わった。

Wasure bana

    robō no ishi no

        katawara ni

The unseasonable blossoming

    of the flower in winter

        stands by the stone on the roadside

Season word: *wasure bana* (*lit.*, "forgotten flower" refers

to the unseasonable blossoming of a flower in winter;

winter)

This allude to the semi-autobiographical novel *Robō no ishi*

(A Stone by the Roadside, 1937–1940) by Yamamoto Yūzō

(1887–1974), which was unfinished due to censorship.

紅葉散る

　　　「色は匂へど

　　　　　散りぬるを」

もみじちる

　　　「いろはにおえど

　　　　　ちりぬるを」

季語　紅葉散る（もみじちる、冬）

以前は、「いろはにほへと」を「色は匂へど散りぬるを、、、」

と謳って覚えた。

Momoji chiru

Iro wa nioe do

chiru nuru o

The maple leaves are falling

reciting the poem

"Their color is sending forth the fragrance,

but the leaves have fallen . . ."

Season word: *momiji chiru* (falling maple leaves; winter)

"I-ro-ha-ni-ho-he-to . . ." is a poem in the form of a perfect

pangram and a traditional Japanese ABCDE, which is still

in use; for instance, C major is referred to as "Ha" major in

music.

冬桜

　　命の鼓動

　　　小刻みに

ふゆざくら

　　いのちのこどう

　　　こきざみに

季語　冬桜（フユザクラ、冬）

フユザクラの花は一重で白色。萼筒（がくとう）は紅色で太

め。冬季から３月まで咲く。

Fuyu zakura

inochi no kodō

kokizami ni

The winter cherry blossoms

their hearts beat

small and fast

Season word: *fuyu zakura* (winter cherry blossoms; winter)

Winter flowering cherry trees have single-petalled pale

pink blossoms, which turn white, looking feeble.

忘れ花

　　流離ひ人の

　　　　擦れし靴

わすればな

　　さすらいびとの

　　　　すれしくつ

季語　忘れ花（わすればな、冬に咲く時ならぬ花、冬）

Wasure bana

    sasurai bito no

       sureshi kutsu

The unseasonable blossoming of the flower in winter

    the worn-out shoes

       of the wanderer

Season word: *wasure bana* (*lit.*, "forgotten flower" refers

to the unseasonable blossoming of a flower in winter;

winter)

About the author

Mayumi Itoh is a former Professor of Political Science at the University of Nevada, Las Vegas (UNLV). She has previously taught at Princeton University and Queens College, City University of New York (CUNY), and has written many academic journal articles and books. Her book titles include:

–*Globalization of Japan: Japanese Sakoku Mentality and U.S. Efforts to Open Japan* (1998)

–*The Hatoyama Dynasty: Japanese Political Leadership Through the Generations* (2003)

–*Japanese War Orphans in Manchuria: Forgotten Victims of World War II* (2010)

–*Japanese Wartime Zoo Policy: The Silent Victims of World War II* (2010)

–*The Origin of Ping-Pong Diplomacy: The Forgotten Architect of Sino-U.S. Rapprochement* (2011)

–*Pioneers of Sino-Japanese Relations: Liao and Takasaki* (2012)

–*Hachi: The Truth of the Life and Legend of the Most Famous Dog in Japan* (2013)

–*The Origins of Contemporary Sino-Japanese Relations: Zhou Enlai and Japan* (2016)

–The Making of China's War with Japan: Zhou Enlai and Zhang Xueliang (2016)

–The Making of China's Peace with Japan: What Xi Jinping Should Learn from Zhou Enlai (2017)

–"Hachi-ko" in Siberia: The True Story of Japanese Prisoners of War and a Dog (2017)

–Hachiko: Solving Twenty Mysteries about the Most Famous Dog in Japan (2017)

–Eliza Ruhamah Scidmore and Japan: The Life and Journeys to the Far East of the American Woman Who Brought "Sakura" to Washington, D.C. (2017)

–Kaneko Misuzu: Life and Poems of A Lonely Princess (2018)

–The Japanese Culture of Mourning Whales: Whale Graves and Memorial Monuments in Japan (2018)

–Animals and the Fukushima Nuclear Disaster (2018)

–Haikus of All Seasons, Vol. I–Vol. X (2018–2019)

–Poems of Kaneko Misuzu and Haikus Inspired by Them, Vol. I–Vol. IV (2019)